I Am a Fact
Not a Fiction

I Am a Fact
Not a Fiction

∽

Selected Poems

by

Edward Mycue

Cover Art

by Richard Steger

Published in 2009 as an online chapbook at:
www.echapbook.com/poems/mycue

Print edition: 2023

ISBN: 978-1-941066-64-5

Cover art: Richard Steger

Book design: Jo-Anne Rosen

Wordrunner Press
Petaluma, California

For Richard Steger

"Two trees have been growing together

For years now.

    ....

During the spring, the waiting

For each the waiting is painful."

— Agnes McGaha, "Stair-Step Wit," from *Two Trees*, page 16, Norton-Coker Press, San Francisco, California, 1991

Contents

HISTORIES

War and Peace

After Time Is Ripe It Is Banished

Root did not eat down.

Now sit, judge.
Now the sky begins to split open.
Other than this is not now.
I do not know other than this.
Other: there where we are not.
Now, here is.

Nuclear swords, dialectic knots hang over
    candidates for Alexander's shoes,
stare-into futures for accidents from yesterday's
    tapestry.

Rot eats down, seasons scatter.
And we read in them, fraying.

Black mirrors, white minutes manure to loam.
Meat is absurd.
Of is from's motive; what is why's dance.

Ideas, nuclear ripe, coral mouthed, are blind windows.
Now sit in judgment on the past and out of that
    dark doorway
remember now is not elsewhere, we are not there
and do not know an elsewhere.

Now here is.
Other: there where we are not.
I do not know other than this.
Other than this is not now.
Now the sky begins to split open.
Now sit, judge.

Snowblood

Burbling up through white
flattened Christ—
massy
crusted
hundred
inches of powdery snow

pillowing up around
the brown trunks
those thousands
of fir, pine, spruce
holly and yew
rises
a deep, warm

red shame of conquest
empire rising
to replace
a republic crucified

democracy became
a snowman
a showman

a deathmask
of snowblood.

Blood Enemy

The enemy of my enemy
is my friend. The friend
of my enemy is my enemy.

The friend of my friend is
my friend (unless that
friend is a friend of the
friend of my enemy). The

feud of my family is
a breach in the friendship
of my blood. My blood is

my enemy? Is this the edge
of my world? How canine
is the tooth of my despair?
Where is a pulse for peace?

A Century Is a Skull Factory

I

It's another century, careless, rudderless
when what's next is curtains
riding the night air
and victims living their injuries
sledding along like a shell in a swift stream
the color of coral, of flamingos
transparence twilled over and
intersecting recesses of hurt.

II

Discrete bits of elsewhere become
yellow tulips in a sodden light
that doesn't equal dusk because it's split
from a century like a skull floating like a factory
whose function is clotting
where optimal longings gather under a mask,

III

but first it curdles into a dance
of confusions called a CLINICAL TRIALS, "mono-
therapies" somewhat like
a mobius strip adder doubling on itself
as I sit wanting to fly from my speech into
silent brown eyes
flecked with gold
crosslegged

waiting
drifting on the current
like a flag.

White Noise (Marketing A War)

there's "intellectual freedom"
and
"intellectual property"
and
the embargo and manipulation of both
plus
the attempt to create a hullabaloo
in order
to focus attention (called "a perfect storm")
or at least
a buzz
the way "placement" does
in
a supermarket or a bookstore.

it's a control issue.
it really markets nothingness.
it's a colorless life
all gauded up and inauthentic.
it's trash and white noise

Tale of Outlaws in the Commons
WHITE HOUSE AUGUST 28 1961 50
    AMERICANS AGES TO ABOUT 30
HEAD FOR GHANA FIRST GROUP OUT
    OF PEACE CORPS VOLUNTEERS

Emphasizing peace not valorizing war nor exalting
   conflict

today summer august 6 2009 what is left of them
   now include
the tired, lame, halted waiting for god and some
   dancing bears

but many are still getting into someone's face space
   and roots
as there is a looming deficit of good will since J.F.
   Kennedy

and an abalone moon is sinking into the western
   skyline as
the goodwill-to- the-world is remaindered into
   recontexualization
and sampling and appropriation as heirs to
   Nixon,Regan,Bush.

Those who can't decide what to do could ask an ant
   as Michael Torrice wrote
in Science Now Daily News in its July 22 2009 dot
   org blog

and meanwhile go strawberrying, bake apple pies,
   smell tulips
or try to find a smell plus seek-out insect life of
   Florida

and don't strive really nor sacrifice futile reality, but
    start afresh
and make new friends, renew you inquiring spirit,
    believe tomorrow

the way the defeated in the Pleissy vs.Ferguson
    believed they'd
ultimately defeat that "separate but equal"
    judgement in 1874.

As I write here in Pacific Daylight Time on the San
    Francisco Bay
we humans not just Americans believe the
    downswing will upswing

and now I hear the water sprite's "Song To The
    Moon" for the 4-act opera
RUSALKA by Antonin Dvorak written 108 years
    ago lilting soaring

still hoping for some rightside-up in next year's
    words/another voice
for that drowned maiden and reconciliation and
    end to remorse.

Still seeking an end of the foredefeated, of the
    usurpation and enjoyment
and use/profits of others, establishing the concept of
    'the commons'

because we are all outsiders in a small space as artist
    Richard Steger said
at a poetry reading in San Francisco's Bird &
    Beckett Bookstore.

Now: I've come to the end of my light years,
    recalling Peace Corps time
and an outlaw in the commons of a global village,
    &then/now strike root.

Do I Need a New Story, Victoria

for Alan and Eva Leveton and Victoria Mycue

From many angles, points of viewing, the rainbow is
    there.
I always try to be a glass carnation of perceptions.
My niece Victoria says changing cannot be forced.

You have to be realistic about what you are seeing
trying to accept and understand even when not
    agreeing.

What makes all the colors in rainbows? I don't live
    in the past.
The past lives on in me, many ways of seeing, many
    me's.
I live in the now, but who am I? Stories, some, get
    highlighted.

I have to become realistic about what I am seeing.
Living now, who am I who am influenced by these
    stories.

From each viewing step, something is highlighted.
    And angle.
Some things are obscured when we focus elsewhere.
When what is love is damaged there can be anger,
    eruptions.

I am influenced by other people's stories as other
    peoples do.
Others combine, collide, ally, curdle, become crazed
    in me.

Our grandparents' blossoms. allegiances, angers can
    be we.
You have to be realistic about what you are seeing,
    she says,
trying to accept and understand even when not
    agreeing.

I'd asked if peace was possible, not "were" it possible.
I asked where's a pulse for peace fearing there was
    none.

Eva and Al, dear friends, said peace—she wrote
    "pulse"—
is often hard to find and you had to keep feeling
    around,
gently. Then feel some more. Never give up on the
    double P.

Victoria, dear niece, says be realistic about your
    seeing,
trying accepting, understanding even when not
    agreeing.

Life / Time / Memory

Cell Damage

Fury injustice abyss ashes
All the animals
Forgetfulness
Innocent beasts
Wild horses wild water
Splash flesh tackle
I drag land
Fierce horses

Terrible beings from below
Get rid of the bones
Snapping sounds
Dry cinders
Pests is what our worth is
Weight and curses
Scurrying rats
Broken back

Such are the birth tales

Translucence

as we rose, we changed — birthslug, toddler,

kiddo, preteen brainiac out through serious
awkwardness, bootielateral-liciously present

into some normatively developed willfullness
termed "transom," "conduit" — symbols for such

flowering forms transversing to any seedy end.

the who we were and are will swell, seek, range,
swim within the scale our mature notions permit

wading through them conducting translucent lives.

Slap My Eyes

i know you are supposed to say you thought it
      would be easier than this (given all strived and
      labored for), and where is the sweet leisured
      payoff. (it is still "in the mail" and "the sun will
      come out tomorrow/ tomorrow/bet your bottom
      dollar...come what may").

that's life: when you come up for air you find you
      are underwater.
there's no retreating back up the birth canal.
amid all the plod 'n grovel there has to be a secret
      santa.

well enough soon enough then enough. enough?
the where's and the when's keep turning.
we are like that teenager in the gulf of aden clinging
      to the airbuss wreckage.

hang in there,
help is on the way.
or maybe sometimes help is in the way.

keep the hope light on.

love is what the clouds send your way

living today yesterday.

Valleys of Departure

As in November when we plant
tulip, hyacinth and daffodil
(pointing
as old bonds grown dull
among mutable
imaginary satisfactions,
like those meiotic moments
in dreamed carts of hay)
those things remembered
trail, reflect
attractions.
The torpor brought
from the soft thocking
has gone and left us only us.
It is time and nothing waits.
It is soon and nothing waits.
It is late and nothing waits.

The Great Wave

This is bitter
Life is brief
Friendships passing
Time's the thief

Life is bitter
This is brief
Passing friendships
Surpassed by grief

Time is liquid
Each sun sets
Sunset renews
Our floating leaf

mood is

a mind-map as if the mind covered
the whole body and its feeling and emotions.

the state of the world
and our u.s.a. contribution
of messing it up has me brooding.

those wasp galls sometimes
ping pong ball size
(and sometimes more tiny than a pea)
on numerous kinds of oak trees
mirror me to myself the way that
"power of ten" idea of out-of-the-body
visualizations re-imagines me to me.
zooming in/out from insignificance
and responsibility to not even
the painted face of a clown.

Knowledge of a Single Rose

The five-petaled regular corolla rose
has sorghum fingers that play with your nose
from the inner envelope. This is not
the Rose of Sharon: that spindling hollyhock
is as near to a rose as a hemlock.

The rosary is a Roman Catholic devotion
that has five sacred "mysteries" and five
sets of ten "decades" of Ave Maria prayers
and each begins with an Our Father prayer,
and each decade ends with the Glory Be one.

It's all repeated like the rose, like some
magical-mystical charm or enchantment "OM."
It's meant as more a path than a pastime:
each rose a single step pilgrimage, window,
colored hope, and compass pleasingly rote.

I know you now, rose; I know you not, rose.

We Remember Magnolia

Trip down memory lane.
In deed. Last year's magnolia.
Time machines march on.
View the past. Only.
Scanning for answers.
For suggestions.
If any are disclosed or uncovered.
The machine never talks "future."
Only scans backward.
Without any updates.
And the time machine memory
only blurs the velvet picture
in any future re-scan backward
because the most recent past
is the foggiest of what was
(having no historical certainty
validated by memory because
those mists seem more real
than today's blindered confusions
we stumble in right now).
Magnolia once white darkens.
But we remember how it was.

Yesterdreams—Star Light

for Chandan Bono

— bronzed pair of booties holding down a sagging
    telephone line,
— picture from a gone time but one that is still just
    out my window
here on fulton and octavia streets next to olive trees
    with plastic bags caught in them
— "witches cowls" — filled with passing breezes

amid caws of crows & occasions when sea birds
    escape east from ocean storms & west
to California from the Sierras when calmer,

settling in our parking lots deciding maybe east or
    west again, birds moving, passing,
pausing; only flitting hummingbirds silent so far

— & my mind's bronzed booties imaged there from
    pairs of tennis shoes often caught on
lines where drug runners marked territories;

my San Francisco mind marked with long densely-
    textured decades written, cared-for, polished,
    discarded, & somehow are written again

because the mind wasn't finished with them & i was
        unable to find a step-down program
to get free from voices, visions. where when i'm

dead will those booties go? will there be telephone
        lines & poles?
will it all sink as sediment under risen shores
        scraped, lathered by

empowered tides with only birds on their ways in
        their days that alone continue while
below fish swim above our yesterday silt

in fogs, rain, wind & sun without anyone until
        "time" arrives as
earth itself fractures into "space" that collides
        beyond my deeming.

Everything Is Bending

Paths lead up, down. Day's not east. All's traffic.
In these necessary hours, a man lifts his arms,
stretching a ready, signaling crimson. A long

shadow adds you. The you adds with. And all
night, love. Bending everything. So, if numbers
inquire, tell them we are the ones, they are ones,

I am one: awe-filled not a turned-brain knob.
If the numbers inquire, tell me you are a one, I
am your one, we truckle, burnished, roan now, in
submarine confusion, swollen, last guest, happy
proclaiming life is the insult. Even when it's not.
If the numbers inquire, you can say how differing

drummers relive, repeat lessons of pilgrimage,
malaise, the hungering decline of allegiances,
how to fill a numb center, to reshape the line.

Night is a dream and I am dreamt by trees. Trees
are like words. Words are veils. In the forests,
the stones are moss-covered. The trees sign to the
    stones.

Between two there are lichens. Between things, words.
Words are the things. But we don't grow wise. Last
night, trees dreamt me, you took me into your arms.

The chill on the night is a path. We don't grow wise.
Hold me. Night is a dream. Permission varies, a person
changes, no fiction's real. The lovers, joined, were

separable. Indistinguishable. Not to themselves: so
neither could extirpate the memory? How could they
be true to their natures? It made them like numbers.

In the jail of San Francisco a gardener's more
    beautiful
than his roses. That odor of decay in tender flesh.
In the Johnny Neptune Bar where the Sunset guys
    shout
"lemme have a Bud, I need a bud" a man is fucked.
"Queer" is a family where since they spoke the same
language all the people understood each other as they

wandered looking for a land to like. When they found
it, they began to change it into a great decorated city.
With decorated walls, courtyards and a tower to make

them famous as Babel because that beckons a proud
people who although overweened and confounded
    with
a curse of voices were one family of bending numbers.

Here cross-dressing is transpersonal. The drag's hero.
Here the mix and match malebox is full. Check it out
You can't order tools for living. Cross-dressing for

counterfeiters, ersatz, fake, actors, novices, postulants.
Pass. Received, recommended. Each an encore. Awe-
some is not the word. Try another body, try clone, truly

yours, try genetic position, try engineering (impotent
mission) try to change anything. Change your whistle!
Divent, divest, invent, invest, enter the second journey

moving through to dis-embody, trans-body, cross over.
Try to change your lord: memory. Go to another
    planet.
Drag-queen's hero, transpersonal. Check it out. Try.

We Leave Nothing Behind

What we experience we are
Much passes through us
But we leave nothing behind

What we are we are
What we have been is us
What is left is nothing

We leave nothing behind
An earthworm caught in time
Much passes through us

What we have been we were
What is left is nothing
We leave nothing behind

Histories

My Policeman

After that first time, he called me on a snowy night
asked me to come to his apartment for drinks with
him and his mother. I wound up spending the night.
His roommate was another policeman away then.
This other guy was engaged and apparently straight.
They slept on mattresses on J's bedroom floor.
I lay down on the roommate's mattress; soon J was
calling me over to his where he asked me if I kissed.
We became more intimate and asked if I 69'd. Then
"brown me" he said squirming over. But the next
week he accused me of turning him queer, beat me.
I was not naïve: so left Amarillo within the week.
He found I'd gotten a job as a reporter in Dallas and
came to the copy desk at the *Times Herald* alternately
saying he loved me and threatening me. I moved
    again.
One day, years later, that old roommate phoned me in
Boston and told me J had shot himself leaving my
telephone number on a note asking that I be called.
J was 33, Arnie said, was a Korean War vet and had
gotten a B.A. at North Texas in Denton on the
    G.I.Bill.
Arnie said he didn"t know what J's demons were, had
been a good friend, was his best man at the wedding:
Arnie and Maris named their first son, Jay, after him.
Arnie said J had been fired from the Police
    Department

for excessive violence in arrests, a questioned stakeout,
but mainly because of his drunkenness. All through
those years he's mentioned me and kept the photo of
the three of us everywhere he lived next to the bed;
    and
Arnie asked if I would like it. I said "keep it for Jay."

Because You're Not Me

Because you're not me
your clock beats endlessly
a time that's not my way
of a place I don't inhabit
in a you I'll never be.

In a you I'll never be
there is an endlessly mystery
like nothing I can get
which perhaps is not unlike
those things I have.

Those things I have
and other strengths I crave
you have deep in your self
because you're not me.

Come Up and Touch Me

Life is a hair shirt, keep the hope light on.
You never no, you sometimes yes, you
just have to proceed by gosh and by guess.
Like the large commercial washer on the left
life keeps washing washing, won't go to rinse.
Books you order are out of stock, unavailable.

Sneer, scowl, aggrieved, petulant patrons ask
what are the fresh daily specials, soups
and then order cheeseburgers with fries.

If for any reason there is dissatisfaction with
this particular poem or with the paper please
return the numbered page with your complaint.
Returns policy (effective Sept. 1, 1997) covers
all purchases within 14 days in saleable shape
except for study, travel guides and CDs.

Today in survival history Friday July 2, 1982
a North Hollywood truck driver hooked 45
weather balloons to his lawn chair and rose up.
7 deadly sins:pride,greed,lust,envy,gluttony,
anger,sloth plus 7 heavenly virtues:prudence,
temperance,justice,fortitude,faith,hope,charity

Life's tight,fussy,overworked — a watercolor.
Then there is mercy in forgetting for a while.

Sometimes I Think I'll Never Learn Spelling

which is sorting the surrendered
henscratches called letters.
Like good law; and misspelling's like legal
breakdown. So anarchy's some alteration from
    a rule: both breakdown and a change —
    transformation, mutation — some sort of
    alteration seen both as reason and result
—like pink burning to purple
—like the Blade Runner's girl Rachel who though
    biologically-engineered gets conscious
—like Pinocchio crying and becoming a "real live
    boy"
—like having another being growing inside of you
—or altering molecular structure
—or learning your true sexuality
—or entering alternative ports
—or varying dimensionality
: such transformations
and misleadings
are revolutions of accepted arrangements
umlauting different drummers' dancings called
"can't" and change as if misspelling. Or
missed spelling?

Driving and Passengering

I.

she picked me up in her SCION ice-
box-on-its-side hearse with
the side and back windows she had
darkened, like a
limo—for privacy: because it doesn't
have a storage trunk. it's
a nice car to get in and out of: my hips
get frozenup now
some days and that's a good aspect. she
is back in form and
she is a good driver. at least her manner
gives one confidence
that she is even if perhaps she might
not be. but at least i
won't be all crazily in fear before the
final crackup.

II.

(i seem to be becoming a nervous
passenger) (i blame it on
the artist who LOOKS at
EVERYTHING—[i blame a lot of
things on him but never never tell him
UNTIL I SCREAM IT

OUT LOUD SOMETIMES: it's a
spousal thing i am
thinking]—when he drives and i get all
like "hey watch the
road" and then he turns to me and
engages plus keeps looking
at everything and the road too.) (so it's
my problem i know
but also my life and my death and the
heck with it.)

III.
sometimes i think you shouldn't
passenger with the people
you sleep with. but maybe that's just
me. and i only think this
way sometimes. you might say. poor
artist: i recall reading
several times in my life the saying (who
said it?) when i meet
a poet i want to wash. it must be hard for
him having me. of
course it's hard for me, too—and 2
hards make a smile. so it works out

Islands in Middle of Lives

Recall the old Zen story of the person who comes
    to an obstruction right in the middle of
the journey of life and sees three choices
1 attempt to force advance 2 go around 3 turn about
    and go back and maybe find some
other life highway to begin on some other mode.
But person does the zen thing and just sits there
    and meditates; and after some time
notices hot dog stands, vegi bars, shops, bookstalls,
    discos that have been setup by other travelers
    who "paused" and sees they have created a whole
    new community unplanned.
One day person finds a circus nearby and as the
    OMs would have it meets
a lama who sells him the mantra "OM
    PADMOSNISA VIMALE HUM PHAT"/
    it's said in the Ksitigarbha Dascakra Sutra that
    whosoever sees, hears, remembers, or touches
    this prayer
will be purified of negativity and gain freedom from
    rebirth in lower regions.
Person begins to reproduce the mantra on saffron-
    colored strips and then later with pastels (paper,
    cloth, plastic, tin, but not leather) and then with
    more primary colors, also with
light printing on a darker field and sells them
    cheaply at some recitations

(of his life, so far) making many friends including a
    balloonist who offers him a ride up/over
the initial obstruction: and the story that goes on
    from there is one that journeyers may navigate
    for themselves on the river of life when they
    come to an island.

I Am a Fact Not a Fiction

I am a fact, not a fiction
a rite, not a ritual
a progression, not a procedure
a song, not a schedule
I am in my life and I live it
— partake it, enjoy it, wonder at it
I'm green leaves aquiver
red clouds aflutter
whacky as Christopher Smart
talking to cats
and alone in dark forests
in short pants
I am Niagara River crashing
over the Falls
cascading through the gorge
to the Devil's Hole
sweeping into the last Great Lake
— Erie to Ontario—
surging into the great Lawrence
into my mother Atlantic
rising forward & into the clouds
into hurricanes
I cut with the knife of the times
out onto the rocks
the Cape of Good Hope to India
South China Sea
sieving through Oceana's islands

Pacific kingdoms
up past Galapagos north home shore
Mission Rock
San Francisco and my love's bed
I am a fact not a fiction.

About Edward Mycue

San Francisco poet Edward
Mycue was born in Niagara
Falls, New York, and raised
in Texas from age eleven.
He was a Lowell Fellow at
Boston University Graduate
School of Public Relations
and Communications, a
WGBH-TV Boston intern,

a Macdowell Colony Fellow, a Peace Corps teacher
in Ghana, editor at the Norton Coker Press, and
he taught American Literature at the International
Peoples College in Elsinore, Denmark.

His books include *Nightboats, The Singing Man My
Father Gave Me, Root Route and Range: the Song Returns,
Because We Speak the Same Language, The Torn Star, Great
Country, Chronicle, Damage Within the Community,
Edward, No One For Free, Pink Garden BrownTrees,
Mindwalking 1937-2007,* and *Song of San Francisco.*

Magazine publications include *New York Quarterly,
Hanging Loose, Boston Review, Washington Review,
Hawai'i Review, Fence, Open City, Stand, Meanjin,
Outrigger, Malahat, Outrigger, Il Signale, Arenaria,
Poetry Australia, Nicolau, La Carta Oliver, fieralingue.
it, poetsagainstthewar.org, Amsterdam Quarterly, Poetry
Ireland, Outlaw Poetry* He edited and published *Took*
magazine's 19 issues in 1987.

Also by Edward Mycue

Books and Chapbooks:

Damage Within the Community, 1973

Chronicle, 1974

Root, Route and Range, 1977

Root, Route and Range: The Song Returns, 1979

The Singing Man My Father Gave Me, 1980

No One For Free, 1984

The Singing Surgeon, 1984

Unity, 1984

Edward, 1985

Idolino, 1985

It's a Grate Country (with Lainie Duro), 1985

The Torn Star, 1986

Pink Garden, Brown Trees, 1990

Because We Speak the Same Language, 1994

Life Is Built From The Inside Out
(with poet Jim Watson-Gove), 1996

Night Boats, 2000

I Am a Fact Not a Fiction (eChapbook edition), 2009

Song of San Franciso, 2012

Anthologies:

Male Muse, 1973

14 Voices, 1975

Anthologies *(continued):*

For David Gasgoyne, 1983

Rhysling, many times between 1987 and 1998

Poly, 1989

Round Glow of Family Nest, 1991

Terminal Velocities, 1992

How the Net is Gripped, 1993

Minotaur, #63, "Beyong the Source," an internal chapbook, pp. 42-75, 2012

Thank you to all of the many magazines and literary journals that have published Ed's work.

Made in the USA
Monee, IL
31 October 2023

45497779R00033